W9-AFX-943

:ure quotations are taken from the Holy Bible, New Interna-
‑sion®. NIV®. Copyright © 1973, 1978, 1984 by Biblica, Inc.™
permission of Zondervan. All rights reserved worldwide. www
ın.com

ٔNUTE PRAYERS® is a registered trademark of The Hawkins Chil-
C. Harvest House Publishers, Inc., is the exclusive licensee of the
registered trademark ONE-MINUTE PRAYERS.

s taken from *One-Minute Prayers™ for Healing* by Hope Lyda and
ıte Prayers™ for Those Who Hurt by Hope Lyda.

Bryce Williamson

ıotos © Zuki, gaga vastard / Getty Images

ٔNUTE PRAYERS® FOR HOPE AND COMFORT
ıt © 2014 by Hope Lyda
ı by Harvest House Publishers
Oregon 97408
ʻvesthousepublishers.com

ʒ-0-7369-7496-7 (Milano Softone™)
ʒ-0-7369-7497-4 (eBook)

in China

22 23 24 25 26 27 / RDS-JC / 10 9 8 7 6 5 4 3 2 1

ONE-MINUT[E]

PRAYE[RS]

for Hop[e]
and Comf[ort]

Hope Ly[...]

HARVEST HOUSE PUB[LISHERS]
EUGENE, OREGO[N]

ON[E...]
Cop[...]
Pub[...]
Euge[...]
www[...]

ISBN[...]
ISBN[...]

Print[ed...]

20[...]

Contents

A Refuge of Peace 5

Stillness 7
Trust 13
Ease 19
Tomorrow 25
Forgiveness 31
Health 37
Protection 43
Rest 49
Holding On 55
Renewal 61
Sanctuary 67
Resurrection 73
Connection 79
Brokenness 85
Fragile 91
Loneliness 97
Motion 103
Healing 109
Excuses 115
Love 121
Peace 127
Meaning 133
Reaching 139
Giving and Receiving 145
Wholeness 151
Belief 157
Joy 163
Discovery 169

A Refuge of Peace

A journey of loss, grief, trial, or busyness can make you weary, physically and spiritually. When words cannot describe your difficulties or sorrows, God still understands just what you need. And as soon as you feel the soothing touch of His love, you know your longing for wholeness has not been forgotten.

May this gathering of prayers and encouraging verses lead you ever closer to God's deep compassion.

God, I walk toward You in this time of need. There is great beauty and possibility in Your presence. What a gift it is to be eased into silence. You hear every beat of my heart and You see every need of my life. My healing comes from Your hand, which is open to receive my burdens and to catch my tears. Thank You for holding my hopes, longings, and prayers with such gentle care. Amen.

Stillness

Refreshed Understanding

*Instead, it should be that of your inner self, the
unfading beauty of a gentle and quiet spirit, which
is of great worth in God's sight.*

1 PETER 3:4

~⁓

So much of my worry and stress stems from outside pressures to be, do, or look a certain way. Lord,
refresh my understanding of beauty and success so that
I may see myself and others through Your eyes.

Today the world clamors for my attention, but I
choose to give it to You. I listen for Your quiet voice
and claim Your definition of unfading beauty—that of
a gentle spirit.

Bearing Up, Bearing With

Be completely humble and gentle; be patient, bearing with one another in love.

EPHESIANS 4:2

~⌒~

Be *completely* humble and gentle. Bear with one another in love. How peaceful Your way is! How far it is from the ways of this world. Thank You, Lord, for patiently bearing with me as I struggle to live more like Christ. You are gentle and loving when I fall short. As I face my trial, it is You who speaks with love and kindness to encourage me and to help me stand and bear my part of this load.

May my lesson be found in Your graciousness. Merciful, comforting God, help me uphold others as You do me—always, with no conditions.

Be Still

The LORD will fight for you; you need only to be still.

EXODUS 14:14

～

Lord, in illness, sadness, and life's battles, You are there for me. I don't need to sound the trumpet or send runners to alert You to my needs. I need only be still. It's within that stillness that I can be watchful—an observer and chronicler of Your deeds. It is in stillness that I sense Your presence—personal, magnificent, holy.

Keep the distractions from my mind. Let me experience the stillness that leads to Your presence.

Waiting Before the Lord

Be still before the LORD and wait patiently for him;
do not fret when men succeed in their ways, when
they carry out their wicked schemes.

PSALM 37:7

~

Waiting is so difficult, Lord. Especially during the dry and difficult times. Being still while waiting? Even harder! I want to pace, point out injustices, even question Your ways. But the psalmist says, "Be still *before* the LORD."

I am humbled. When I consciously draw into Your presence, I cannot fret and flail about. Your gentle, patient spirit quiets mine. When indignant words and feelings well up, remind me to draw nigh to You and surrender all my troubled thoughts.

Trust

Never and Forever

Those who know your name will trust in you, for you, LORD, have never forsaken those who seek you.

PSALM 9:10

~ᵒ

Lord, Your very name opens our heart's door to trust. Your name conquers worry. It promises protection to the seeker and fellowship to the finder. I can seek refuge in the comfort and security of Your holy name.

You have never forsaken Your followers, and this is forever true. Praise Your most trustworthy name!

Surely, I Will Sing

Surely God is my salvation; I will trust and not be afraid. The LORD, the LORD, is my strength and my song; he has become my salvation.

ISAIAH 12:2

~⁀

The Lord is my strength and my song. How often I rely on Your strength, Lord, but I forget the song part. I neglect to praise You with the melodies of my heart and voice. I fail to point to You as the source of my trust, joy, and confidence.

I need to sing Your praises in all places so that others will take up Your name, live without fear, and experience the amazing gift of salvation.

Trust's Many Treasures

May the God of hope fill you with all joy and peace as you trust in him, so that you may overflow with hope by the power of the Holy Spirit.

ROMANS 15:13

God of hope, Your promises are many and good. When I let go and trust You with my problems, You send me the solace of peace. When I go about my daily life, enveloped in Your peace, I feel a quiet joy.

When I let go, I am finally able to look up and enjoy the good things You've placed around me. By Your Holy Spirit, I feel hope and renewed strength. God of hope, I pray I am quicker to trust next time.

Here I Am!

Do not let your hearts be troubled. Trust in God;
trust also in me.

JOHN 14:1

~~

When Jesus spoke these words to His disciples,
He was standing bodily before them. "Trust in God,"
He said. "Trust also in me [Jesus]." Like the disciples,
I sometimes need to be reminded of the good things I
have seen in order to trust.

Today I experience You through the Spirit, but I
can testify to the many times You rescued me in very
real, tangible ways. Remind me of this, Lord, when I
begin to think of my faith as a "thing." Remind me that
this journey is a covenanted relationship—not an idea.
"I AM" is here.

Ease

Fearless

Whoever listens to me will live in safety and be at ease, without fear of harm.

PROVERBS 1:33

I can feel my muscles grip with tension and fear each time I think of the uncertain things in my future. It is useless, this worrying. Yet I invest much time and energy toward it. I cannot know what is around the bend, but I am under the care of the one who does know what will come and what will happen.

Lord, Your voice envelops me, and I am ready to listen to Your words of peace and security. You do not reveal secrets of what is to come, but You say, "Continue without fear. We take the next steps together." Thank You for that comfort.

Leaning on You

Trust in the LORD with all your heart and lean not on your own understanding.

PROVERBS 3:5

~⌒

I have tried to stand tall with my feet planted in certainty...but my will is fading, Lord. I look to You and see the pillar of strength and comfort. Your grace rises above my circumstances, and yet You understand my very human worries and anxious moments.

You gather me and my concerns into Your arms. My body melts into the eternal grip of Your sovereign embrace. I don't need to pretend to be brave or all-knowing. My resistance and pride give way to understanding all I need to know...You are here for me.

Waiting for the Light

For my yoke is easy and my burden is light.

MATTHEW 11:30

Okay, Lord. I'm ready to share this with You. I know I have said it before, but this time I mean it. Last time I held on to a little bit here and a little bit there. You showed me that my faith was halfhearted. The child in me wanted to cling to what I knew best, but I was only making it harder on myself.

Lord, this time the situation is Yours to mold, shape, pare down, and whatever else needs doing. I give You my heart and, in return, You give me a life that is eased by love and grace. You lighten my load so that I can follow You with sure steps. Thank You.

How Good You Are

Then the LORD God provided a vine and made it grow up over Jonah to give shade for his head to ease his discomfort, and Jonah was very happy about the vine.

JONAH 4:6

~

You have blessed me in mighty ways, Lord. While I sweat and toil and whine and cry and rebel against possible discomfort, You are shaping something new and wonderful in my life. It will grow out of this situation, and it will gain strength from my weakness. This new creation will wind its way around the framework of my days and blossom with fragrant fruit.

I stand beneath this vine of goodness and abundance, and my eyes are shaded from the sweltering sun. I can see the lush horizon ahead of me.

Tomorrow

I Wouldn't Dream of It

Do not boast about tomorrow, for you do not know what a day may bring forth.

PROVERBS 27:1

~

I have given up guessing what is in store for me, Lord. I used to think I had life all figured out. I thought I understood Your ways completely. But that was ignorance on my part. Forgive me for the times I bragged about what my path would become.

Lord, I no longer believe I own today or tomorrow. They are Yours alone to shape and to give. I wouldn't dream of filling my days predicting what will happen next. And You don't ask me to. You only ask that I trust You with every breath, every today, and every tomorrow.

My Story's Legacy

Let this be written for a future generation, that a
people not yet created may praise the Lord.

PSALM 102:18

～

If I tell it well…if I share of the hope I have in You, there will be people around me who also hold onto this hope. In ways I cannot imagine, You will make a legacy out of my story. I am humbled by my circumstances. May Your glory shine brightly in the darkness of my sadness or misfortune.

Give me the courage to never hold back from telling of my frailty or humility. In turn, Your strength will be magnified. 'Tis You who carries me through today. It will be You who ushers me into tomorrow. May those who observe this truth be encouraged.

Tomorrow I Rest

"For I know the plans I have for you," declares the
LORD, "plans to prosper you and not to harm you,
plans to give you hope and a future."

JEREMIAH 29:11

Today is about perseverance. Holding my head up.
Keeping things in order at work and home when I
would rather nap or holler at the sky. Today is about
smiling when I would rather cry; ignoring indifference
when I crave attention.

Today is about moving forward with my eyes
focused on the future rather than the past. Today is
about working through whatever You place on my
plate so that I can rest tomorrow. Your plan will not
break me. It will guard my steps so that I can take
refuge in the hopeful future You declare for me, Your
child.

Guard My Worries

*Therefore do not worry about tomorrow, for
tomorrow will worry about itself. Each day has
enough trouble of its own.*

MATTHEW 6:34

Each morning my problems are opened up slowly
and deliberately. One by one I lift the difficulties up to
the light, examine them, and decide what to do. But
there are more problems than time. It seems I have
tomorrow's troubles in with today's batch.

Lord, I'm getting it. I'm grasping Your provision and
the lessons I am to learn. I will unwrap only those decisions, choices, and hurdles for today. The others that
remain in my mind and on my heart will be wrapped
tightly and handed back to You for safekeeping. Hold
them please. I will not give them a moment's worry
today.

Forgiveness

I Speak Your Name

For the sake of your name, O LORD, forgive my iniquity, though it is great.

PSALM 25:11

~⁀

You speak my name. I have heard it on the wind, beneath my own voice, and in my ear when I needed encouragement. Your forgiveness covers me, lifts me up, and pulls me forward. I am so grateful. Your grace is mighty, Lord, and it is given to me with love.

I speak Your name, Lord, because this is a time of praise. Thank You for spreading Your arms wide and accepting all of me—including the hurts, the complaints, the tender places of pride, the sins, and the flaws.

You Are the Source

For if you forgive men when they sin against you,
your heavenly Father will also forgive you.

MATTHEW 6:14

~

It is from You, the source of all that is good and holy, that I am finally able to draw the strength to forgive those who cause me pain. Some know they have hurt me; some don't. Some are not in the wrong, yet I want to blame them.

I finally realized that my anger turned me away from the well of forgiveness often. But You called me to return with the pail of my heart. You asked me to lean over, extend the vessel, and fill it because the supply from You is endless. Now I am more eager to return to Your heart and draw my reserve of forgiveness. I want to share it with everyone.

Grudges

And when you stand praying, if you hold anything against anyone, forgive him, so that your Father in heaven may forgive you your sins.

MARK 11:25

~

I like peace. But lately I seem to foster angst. I turn negative comments over and over in my mind. Other people's sins become something for me to figure out, to change, to make right. Lord, I'm pretty sure You have not asked me to take Your place as God, Creator, and Savior! So why do I try to be the one in ultimate control?

I allow hurts to fester and slights to separate me from Your goodness. Release me from the grudges that keep my heart in shackles. Give me the strength to release the desire to control everyone and everything.

Formula for Forgiveness

Do not judge, and you will not be judged. Do not condemn, and you will not be condemned. Forgive, and you will be forgiven.

LUKE 6:37

~

Just getting dressed or choosing what to have for dinner can seem difficult these days. So why don't I allow some things to be simple? God, You established an easy formula for us to follow. We are called to give others the forgiveness You give to us. You say we can rest easy and stop being the judge, jury, and condemner.

It would save me time, energy, effort, and patience if I followed this recipe for peace. I don't know if I will have spaghetti or salad tonight, but I know for certain that I will forgive my neighbor, my friend, the driver in the other lane, and anyone You bring into my life that needs it. It's that simple.

Health

A Balm of Kindness

*Pleasant words are a honeycomb, sweet to the soul
and healing to the bones.*

PROVERBS 16:24

∼

Oh, how I long for kind sentiments and gentle expressions. Lord, give me healing words through others, Scripture, and in my own thoughts. Difficult conversations or worrisome discussions of tasks and to-do lists feel harsh and abrasive to my tender soul. I don't have the energy for this.

May I find sweetness in every exchange. May I listen for encouraging comments. May I learn to lift up prayers and praises to You and fill my own speech with words that offer hope and comfort.

What Healing Looks Like

Nevertheless, I will bring health and healing to it; I will heal my people and will let them enjoy abundant peace and security.

JEREMIAH 33:6

~

I want to be whole, Lord. Instead, I feel broken in places. My heart is shattered and slowly, slowly mending. Some mornings I barely have energy to get up. All along I have had this picture of absolute healing and health. It is a perfect picture filled with a flawless, energized version of myself.

But, God, I was forgetting the healing I experienced to get to this place. I had forgotten to look behind me and notice how far I have come. More and more I experience moments of peace and trust in Your ways. These snapshots of time make up the picture of healing. They shape the image of hope in my heart.

Most Sacred

Above all else, guard your heart, for it is the well-spring of life.

PROVERBS 4:23

～

Lord, You know me. You know how I tend to retreat when I face trials of this sort. I distance myself from others to protect my feelings and my energy. During my times of solitude and separation, You make my heart a place to rest, a sanctuary to gather my senses and to experience calm. Here I can draw from Your strength, hear Your voice, and feel safe.

Let me cherish this sacred place and preserve it so that it remains a pure connection to my Creator.

Thank Goodness

Reckless words pierce like a sword, but the tongue
of the wise brings healing.

PROVERBS 12:18

I was leaning toward negative talk. I started to speak of the worst case scenario again. But a friend spoke wisdom into my life. This friend cleared away the cobwebs of old thinking. How close I was to giving my hope over to unbelief.

Lord, thank goodness I heard Your words of healing and health come from another. I needed them. I longed for truth to counter my false ideas. Wisdom is a foundation that will hold me up, even when I am weak.

Protection

What I Have

May integrity and uprightness protect me, because
my hope is in you.

PSALM 25:21

~

My hurt is becoming apparent to others. Several have mentioned it, and I was surprised. My situation feels so personal that I believed it existed only in my thoughts, in my experience. But others know of my pain. I pray they do not begin to see me as what I have lost, rather than as Your child.

God, give me a continued desire to serve You with integrity. Protect my intention to be a witness. Make my life an example of Your glory, Your goodness, and Your faithfulness. And when others mention my situation, may they always use the word "hope."

Seeking Refuge

*You are my hiding place; you will protect me from
trouble and surround me with songs of deliverance.*

PSALM 32:7

~

Cover me, Lord. Be my protector and my protection. Save me from despair. Keep me from my deep night worries and my daylight stresses. Guard my heart and my life from falseness and trouble. Prepare me today for whatever You call me to do tomorrow.

Lord, I lean on You and Your strength for everything I do. Only when I step toward You do I hear the song of deliverance, the notes of a future hope.

Until I Think

Discretion will protect you, and understanding will guard you.

PROVERBS 2:11

～ᵕ

I have a hard time holding back the thoughts that want to pour forth every day. My current pain has become a truth serum of sorts. I want to blurt my feelings about everything all the time. I lack discretion because I'm wearing my heart on my sleeve.

Hold me and my tongue, Lord. Keep me from wandering away from the path You have for me. Save me from myself and my desire to blurt out the raw emotions that well up inside. It is not that I cannot speak these parts of my soul, but You call me to share them with You first because You protect me.

Always True

But the Lord is faithful, and he will strengthen and protect you from the evil one.

2 THESSALONIANS 3:3

~

When the lies of deception envelop me, I doubt all that I have, all that I am, and worst of all...all that You are. When my loss or hurt seems insurmountable, I wonder who I am and who cares for me. As sorrow covers me, I lose sight of the colors You have painted across the sky and the land.

God, You are faithful. I say this not to make it true, but to bring truth back to my perspective. I know that this is always fact. When I am weak, You are strong.

Rest

Have God, Will Travel

*The LORD replied, "My Presence will go with you,
and I will give you rest."*

EXODUS 33:14

~⁀

I built so many walls around myself that my home seemed a palace, a refuge that should not be left behind. I made excuses for my behavior and told myself and others that being alone was the healthiest solution. Lord, You call me out of my solitary confinement. You promise to give me rest and refreshment even when I leave this refuge.

Today I will step forward with new assurance and confidence. Today I will stop hiding and begin living in Your care. Today I will acknowledge Your presence and celebrate the comfort You bring. There will be no more walls. I will step beyond them and begin living because You are my Savior.

Scanning the Horizon

But now the LORD my God has given me rest on
every side, and there is no adversary or disaster.

1 KINGS 5:4

～

I'm still looking for what might happen next. What trouble awaits me around this corner or behind this decision? Who is preparing to bring me bad news this very moment? Lord, I am struggling to take a breath even when You give me room to breathe. My doubts fill every crevice of this life. I want to purge them from this time. I want to believe.

Thank You for this time of solace and silence. Give me the courage to rest in it as a believer. May this be a time for me to restore my hope in You.

Where Can I Sit?

My soul finds rest in God alone; my salvation comes from him.

PSALM 62:1

~⌒⌒

It's as if I have been playing musical chairs for a year. But my reflexes are slow and my instincts wrong. I never get a chair. I stand. I wait for the music to begin again. My feet are tired, my head hurts, my heart aches, and all I want is to sit for a few moments and regain my bearings.

You saw me standing in the center of the circle looking dazed. Lord, You offered me Your chair, a place by Your side, and a chance to recover. I shed tears when You bent down to wash my feet. I could not stop crying because of the love and relief. This is what resting in You feels like.

As Close as a Memory

Be at rest once more, O my soul, for the LORD has been good to you.

PSALM 116:7

~

I stepped out into the sunshine and thought nothing of it. I sipped delicious coffee and commented that it was too hot. I accomplished a feat today that I have been trying to do for months...and a friend had to point it out to me. I have forgotten how to live with joy.

Lord, I stop in this moment and think back to a time of joy. It was not so long ago in days, but in the emotional journey it was an eternity. I stood straight and sure. Your love was all around me. I felt its warmth, I tasted its sweetness, and I celebrated the success. My soul reaches through the numbness. Lord, You have been good to me.

Holding On

Something to Believe

Therefore, my dear brothers, stand firm. Let nothing move you. Always give yourselves fully to the work of the Lord, because you know that your labor in the Lord is not in vain.

1 CORINTHIANS 15:58

~

I have a stack of how-to books...not for home improvement but for life improvement. I've tried a few of those ideas. I gave a couple of those steps a chance. I even did a few of the top 10 ways to a better life. But it seemed all for naught. Then I realized I was not making an investment in Your work. Laboring in Your will offers a sure return of goodness, wholeness, and purpose.

Let me stand firm in the work that comes from Your hand. Today my job is to experience trust and belief and to hold on to the hope of Your promises. This is not in vain.

Watching the Tide

*Timothy, my son, I give you this instruction in
keeping with the prophecies once made about you,
so that by following them you may fight the good
fight, holding on to faith and a good conscience.
Some have rejected these and so have shipwrecked
their faith.*

1 TIMOTHY 1:18-19

~

The waves reach the sky today. I cannot see past
them to what is next. You have given me a vessel in
which to ride out these waters. Fear restricts my heart,
but I stay on course. I gave up steering long ago. This
life and my future are in Your hands.

I have armed myself with maps and notes from the
journeys of others. Yet all along I have only needed to
hold on to faith. As the waves subside momentarily,
I see that I am perfectly in line with the course You
charted for me long ago. I should not be surprised, but
relief floods my heart once again.

Sure, But Can You Do This?

Test everything. Hold on to the good.

1 THESSALONIANS 5:21

~

In my need, I have reached for many lifelines. I am embarrassed to confess, Lord, that I sought out help that was not of Your strength. What was I thinking? How weak is my resolve to be solid in my faith and my commitment to You!

I was forgetting how committed You are to me. I don't deserve this grace, this mercy from You. Nevertheless, You give it to me with love and guidance. You don't shame me for trying to be strong on my own. But I sense that You smile like a knowing parent when I return, once again, to take hold of Your wisdom and call it the only true lifeline.

Me?

Be patient, then, brothers, until the Lord's coming.
See how the farmer waits for the land to yield
its valuable crop and how patient he is for the
autumn and spring rains. You too, be patient and
stand firm, because the Lord's coming is near.

JAMES 5:7-8

~

How many friends have I witnessed to about the virtues of waiting upon Your timing? Countless. Not long before my trial came into my life, I was talking about this very thing. I'm sure I said it with great authority and conviction. I was good at that then.

Now I stand in my living room with my hands held up to the ceiling. I have only questions, not conviction, on my lips and on my mind: "When will You take this from me? When will You fix this, Lord?" I feel the tug on my heart almost immediately. It is not judgment, but mercy. "You too must be patient and stand firm." I let this sink in. It isn't a platitude; it's a true answer.

Renewal

A New Being

He saved us, not because of righteous things we had done, but because of his mercy. He saved us through the washing of rebirth and renewal by the Holy Spirit.

TITUS 3:5

~

My prayer today is that this time of enduring, waiting, and hoping will lead to a rebirth. I truly believe that I can never return to my old way of living and thinking. The me that comes out of this birth canal will be shaped by this experience.

My mind returns to the word "renewal" because it refreshes my spirit to think of this possibility. I rest in my salvation. I have witnessed Your mercy, and I wait for the new beginning on the other side of this labor.

Awakening

Create in me a pure heart, O God, and renew a steadfast spirit within me.

PSALM 51:10

~⌒⁓

Give me a pure heart for You, Lord. Place in my life a genuine goodness that comes from Your mercy. As I face hurt, let me find ways to share a spirit of fellowship, faith, and love with others. I want the great things to shine so brilliantly that they distract me from my pain.

This time in my life once felt like a time of slumber, of closing, of restriction. Only now am I seeing that it is a time of renewal, creation, opening, and abundance. May I keep my heart in this place of awareness and awakening so that I do not miss what You are sharing with me.

Not So Long Ago

Even youths grow tired and weary, and young men stumble and fall; but those who hope in the LORD will renew their strength. They will soar on wings like eagles; they will run and not grow weary, they will walk and not be faint.

ISAIAH 40:30-31

~⌒

Not so long ago I was strong and resilient. My limbs could stretch, reach, and pull me forward. My laughter was uncensored and vibrant. Not so long ago I did not know what time and trial would bring my way.

Now You tend to my wounds, Lord. When I fall to my knees, You reach for me and help me continue with this day, this task, and this trial. Each time I lean upon Your might, I feel lighter, more able, and more free. Not so long ago I would have naively credited this renewal to my own strength rather than to my hope in You. Thank You for opening my eyes.

New Thoughts

Be transformed by the renewing of your mind.
Then you will be able to test and approve what
God's will is—his good, pleasing and perfect will.

ROMANS 12:2

~

I'm ready to exchange my old thoughts for new ones. God, please edit my mind's offerings...they are negative, worldly, and most of the time quite scrambled. I need clarity and direction. I am not able to measure my perception against Your truth because I have lost my way.

God, transform my thoughts, my feelings, and my outlook on life right now. I need to see what could be and what is through the lens of possibility and eternity. Only then will I see the view You have created for me. Only then will the words that fill my mind be from Your heart.

Sanctuary

Moving In

LORD, who may dwell in your sanctuary? Who may live on your holy hill?

PSALM 15:1

～

I've felt alone in my struggle lately. I am not always good at letting people in. I keep a safe distance from those who might ask how I am. Yet I am sad when others do not reach out to me. Lord, I'm tired of being alone in this. I need the chance to depend on others... and especially on Your strength.

I'm ready to move into Your sanctuary. I want to bring my soul, my heart, my troubles, my baggage, my wounds, and my hope and make my home in the refuge of Your love.

Storing Up

You are awesome, O God, in your sanctuary;
the God of Israel gives power and strength to his
people. Praise be to God!

PSALM 68:35

~

The many years I have loved You and praised You are a source of power for me now. When I awaken in the middle of the night to the sound of my heart pounding, I draw from my past experiences of faith to calm me. I reflect on Your goodness and the certainty of Your faithfulness I have witnessed in my life and in the lives of others.

You are awesome. My hurts seem so big, so deep… but so is Your embrace. I am thankful for the years I have trusted You. Help me to continue my end of this covenant, Lord. Let me be a person who seeks and knows the sanctuary of faith intimately.

Resurrection

What You Ask

"Lord," Martha said to Jesus, "if you had been here, my brother would not have died. But I know that even now God will give you whatever you ask."

Jesus said to her, "Your brother will rise again."

Martha answered, "I know he will rise again in the resurrection at the last day."

Jesus said to her, "I am the resurrection and the life. He who believes in me will live, even though he dies; and whoever lives and believes in me will never die. Do you believe this?"

"Yes, Lord."

JOHN 11:21-27

~

I have known others who have been raised out of their adversity, loss, or addiction. Yet my first impulse is to say, "Lord, if You had been here, I would not have fallen into despair." But, of course, You were here. You are here. And You extend Your power of resurrection and life in ways I have not given myself over to. You ask, "Do you believe?" And I am raised from my pit of doubt enough to see that my hurt is not eternal—You are.

Wrong Direction

Why do you look for the living among the dead?
He is not here; he has risen!

LUKE 24:5-6

~~

This week I have been wallowing a bit. I didn't want to get up off the couch. Sometimes I feel this way—so lost. I started examining my past and wondering what I had done to deserve this difficulty. I scanned the years and the memories to see if there was a solution. But I was looking for signs of life among the dead and gone.

Lord, lift me up. Let my thoughts and my mood and my attitude rise up with You, the resurrected Christ. When I start searching the old, the lifeless, turn my attention back to the living God, for my hope is there.

I Need You

*Rise up and help us; redeem us because
of your unfailing love.*

PSALM 44:26

~

In my very core I feel the need for You. Nothing around me is sufficient to ease my concerns. Even my closest friends and their kind comforts do not lessen this deep ache. I am craving time with You. When I pray, a sweet peace covers me like the most luxurious blanket. I curl up to become more and more protected by Your love.

May I return to this sense of need often. It brings me closer to Your heart. Safe in Your embrace, I do not question the concept of unfailing love, I welcome it.

Into the Hope

Praise be to the God and Father of our Lord Jesus Christ! In his great mercy he has given us new birth into a living hope through the resurrection of Jesus Christ from the dead.

1 PETER 1:3

~⁀

I'm stepping forward. Slowly and with deliberate steps, but still forward. It has been a long time since I have felt any sense of progress. Thank You, Lord, for this gift of life. I can breathe more easily this morning. My thoughts are clear and fresh. I look around me and everything is vibrant, colorful, alive. It is as if You are pointing out all that I have missed in the past days and weeks.

Yes, today I am stepping into a living hope and a hope for living.

Connection

A Part

*Finally, all of you, live in harmony with one
another; be sympathetic, love as brothers,
be compassionate and humble.*

1 PETER 3:8

~

I have been disconnected from the body of Christ.
I am living apart from others even though I interact
with people every day. My hurts are causing me to turn
away. I spoke with someone who has many burdens,
and I felt overwhelmed, unable to reach out of my own
pain to ease that of another.

Lord, I want to be whole and a part of the whole
body. As I thirst for compassion, may I also draw from
the well of Your mercy to gather compassion to extend
to others. Humble me during this time so that I might
learn the lesson of generosity.

Inside Out

*I appeal to you, brothers, in the name of our Lord
Jesus Christ, that all of you agree with one another
so that there may be no divisions among you and
that you may be perfectly united in mind and
thought.*

1 CORINTHIANS 1:10

~

God, You call us to be united and in agreement
with one another. Help! I struggle to find common
ground with some people lately. The brokenness inside
of me wants to create division outside of me. Is it
anger? Loneliness? Adversity?

Lord, help me heal within so that I will desire
agreement and unity in my relationships. Where I am
raw, soothe me. Where I am jagged, smooth me. And
where I am shattered, piece me back together. Only
Your holiness will bring my wholeness.

Who Can Handle It?

Be completely humble and gentle; be patient,
bearing with one another in love.

EPHESIANS 4:2

~⁹

Lord, I want to yell. To shout! To cry at the top of my lungs. I don't care who sees how messy I am right now. At least that would feel like an authentic connection with another person. I have been living on autopilot mode and it scares me.

But who, besides You, can handle that kind of outburst from me? Who can see the darker places that I feel and still be able to love me? Lord, show me who can bear this burden with me right now. Give me the courage to reach out to those You place in my path so that I can humble myself and risk being vulnerable with another child of God.

No Comparison

Do not be proud, but be willing to associate with people of low position. Do not be conceited.

ROMANS 12:16

⁓

"My pain is bigger than your hurt." I almost said this to someone today, Lord. In the moment, I actually felt superior to the other person because of my troubles. Or maybe I just thought he could not possibly understand me and what I am going through. I cut him off in his effort to relate when actually I wanted to make a connection.

God, release me from having an identity shaped by my worries. I do long for connection and understanding from others. Help me stop comparing hearts and hurts. Allow me to see each person's value through Your eyes and not my own.

Brokenness

The Rubble of Old Ways

*Like a city whose walls are broken down is a man
who lacks self-control.*

PROVERBS 25:28

~

I feel so vulnerable these days. My fortress of perceived togetherness and success has been destroyed. I step over the rubble that was once a supposedly good life and raise my hands to heaven. What now, Lord? What now?

I trust You to raise up what is truly an honorable, meaningful existence. Out of these ashes and the debris of broken dreams and an adjusted sense of happiness, I ask You to create something wonderful, something that reminds me what true love is.

After the Fall

*The bows of the warriors are broken, but those
who stumbled are armed with strength.*

1 SAMUEL 2:4

~

Lord, You have made the weak strong. Your power
rushes through my veins as I struggle to stand and
face the fight of my trial. There are many mighty warriors about me who seem to manage their way fine.
But I have taken a fall. All that I have worked hard for
crumbles to the ground.

Yet, I also know what it is like to fall into Your
strength—to surrender my will to Your own, to know
that there is a good thing taking shape that I cannot
see right now. You cover me with strength and ability.
You will carry me through the days ahead.

Mending the Break

*You will say then, "Branches were broken off so
that I could be grafted in." Granted. But they were
broken off because of unbelief, and you stand by
faith. Do not be arrogant, but be afraid.*

ROMANS 11:19-20

～

I make room for You in the most indirect ways.
Instead of inviting You into my life, Lord, and asking
You to rule over it with Your love and mercy, I force
the situation. I fail, I stumble, I break off branches of
my life, and then look to You to fix these pieces and
make them stronger. I ask You to mend me so that I
may bear the fruit of righteousness.

I cannot take credit for the times I do rise above
such humbling circumstances. It is Your doing. I pray
to be able to start trusting You from the beginning, to
not require so much mending. I invite You to extend
my branches to reach out in new ways. I stand by faith.

Weak Are Made Strong

But we have this treasure in jars of clay to show that this all-surpassing power is from God and not from us.

2 CORINTHIANS 4:7

⁓

Anyone who knows the past problems in my life is amazed at how You continue to use me...a very broken, weak vessel. I am not whole in the way the world expects, but I am made whole, strong, and redeemable by Your grace. The cracks that other people see only increase the praise and credit I can offer You.

To those who wonder I can say, "See this missing piece? See this shattered bit of pottery? My Potter is still able to fill me with His purpose and call me a worthy vessel." As I speak these words and pray this praise, I thank You, Lord, for calling me beautiful. I am a treasure that desires to be filled again and again.

Fragile

My Favorite Hiding Place

Rescue me from my enemies, O LORD, for I hide myself in you.

PSALM 143:9

~

If these current hurts can be my teachers, they offer me lessons about whom to trust and where to run. I cannot hide from life, though I have tried that during my weakest moments. But I can seek Your shelter when the most difficult enemies start to undermine my purpose. These enemies—fatigue, sorrow, doubt, fragility, stubbornness—seem insurmountable at times, until I can run to You.

Lord, You are my favorite hiding place. You offer a drink to cool me, a bed for rest, and protection against these threats to my life. Soon You will encourage me with words I need to hear. Then I will return to make my way through this circumstance, no longer weary, no longer fearful.

Walking the Valley

*Even though I walk through the valley of the
shadow of death, I will fear no evil, for you are
with me; your rod and your staff, they comfort me.*

PSALM 23:4

～

I am removed from those on the mountain. I look
up and wave or nod to them along their journey. But
I am here in the valley, Lord. This is where lush life
grows, but for me it is a time of sorrow and uncertainty.
I can only glance at those on higher plains once in a
while, because my time here is so burdensome. Each
step I take is my only focus.

But then up ahead I see You standing with Your
rod and staff. You are waiting patiently and pointing
out the secure places to step. I am almost there. Now
we walk together, and You point out a mountain in the
future that will be mine. Your promise to lead me out
of the valley, Lord, is my only focus.

Great Expectations

Watch and pray so that you will not fall into temptation. The spirit is willing, but the body is weak.

MATTHEW 26:41

~

Oh, I am so willing, Lord. My spirit craves to do right. My heart beats so that I may grow to love You more. I pray for my life today and in the days ahead. I know there will be many times when I am tempted to quit the journey, stop caring, fade from my life.

Your love for me is my lifeline during these times. My spirit can cling to You and see the way through simple, everyday circumstances and the most difficult situations. It all feels hard right now, so I will not trust my first physical reaction. I will only trust the pull of my spirit toward Your presence.

Handle with Care

Turn to me and be gracious to me, for I am lonely and afflicted.

PSALM 25:16

Turn to me, Lord. Look at my face. See beyond the eyes, the lines, the signs of fatigue. See through to me. You understand what will raise me from this time. I cannot figure it out, and other people do not know what I need.

Turn to me, Lord. Be gracious to me. My loneliness haunts me. My pain is real. I have nobody to explain it to, figure it out with, who will fully understand. So I keep it all: the loneliness, the pain, the worry. It lies down with me, and even my dreams do not provide distance.

Turn to me, Lord. Let me rest my weary mind and body and spirit in Your presence while You watch over me.

Loneliness

Never Alone

But a time is coming, and has come, when you will be scattered, each to his own home. You will leave me all alone. Yet I am not alone, for my Father is with me.

JOHN 16:32

~

Other people may come and go, leaving the life I know to go on to other things, but this is to be expected. Why, though, does this hurt me so? I take it personally that others are finding their foothold and stepping up or out, and You have called me to remain here alone, figuring it all out slowly and with much trepidation.

I know that I am not alone. I am never alone, for You are with me and You see where I stand. You see my sorrow and the loneliness that fills my days. I do not have a home to return to—not yet. But You prepare a place for me in this life and also in eternity. This is the future home I have to long for. This is the home that draws me back into the shelter of love and comfort.

Wisdom of the Widow

*The widow who is really in need and left all alone
puts her hope in God and continues night and day
to pray and to ask God for help.*

1 TIMOTHY 5:5

~

The loss of what is familiar to me leaves me feeling
alone. God, You care for the most basic of my needs.
I must trust You in the same way a widow does, as if
my life depended on Your provision and mercy. This is
truly a life of faith. When I felt strong and in control,
I was losing sight of how to depend on You and Your
help.

Night and day, I call out my needs to You and wait
for them to be covered. The emptiness in me opens
to the point of pain so that I can receive Your mercy.
I am left alone with my thoughts and emotions, but I
am never left alone in my need. Grant me the ability
to firmly understand and praise You for this difference.

Free in Our Slavery

Though we are slaves, our God has not deserted us in our bondage. He has shown us kindness in the sight of the kings of Persia: He has granted us new life to rebuild the house of our God and repair its ruins, and he has given us a wall of protection in Judah and Jerusalem.

EZRA 9:9

My prison is becoming familiar to me. I fear I might become accustomed to this sense of restriction and poverty and never return to a life where I am free. God, be with me now and teach me the lessons of freedom that You offered slaves and captives—those who were mistreated, abused, and considered less than human.

The secret You offer is hope in the face of indifference, resurrection in the face of death, and peace in the face of hatred. You give new life to those who seek Your face during their unfathomable moments in the pit of despair. You protect the most important part of me, Lord. You know my spirit must rise above these circumstances. Through my spirit, I will forever be free.

Motion

Action

But Jesus immediately said to them: "Take courage! It is I. Don't be afraid." "Lord, if it's you," Peter replied, "tell me to come to you on the water." "Come," he said. Then Peter got down out of the boat, walked on the water and came toward Jesus.

MATTHEW 14:27-29

~⌇

When You call us into action, Lord, it is for our own good. It is a way of moving us forward and toward a future. Because I am so weary, I long to sit. I fantasize about falling into a deep slumber and waking up once this struggle is over. But, Lord, You waken me to the wonder of trusting You.

Help me recognize Your face and Your voice as You call me to take action. What should I do, Lord? Ask it of me, and give me the strength...and the faith...to follow through.

Model Behavior

Whatever you have learned or received or heard from me, or seen in me—put it into practice. And the God of peace will be with you.

PHILIPPIANS 4:9

~

During this time, I have spent moments reflecting on the blessing of those people who model a strong Christian faith. I thank You for the gifts of friends, family members, and strangers who have shown me aspects of Your character. I draw on this heritage when I need to make decisions.

There are days when I am functioning on autopilot. God, I want to surrender my actions to Your will. I want to step out with a strong faith. When I do not know what to do, I will rely on what I have learned, received, and heard from those who have walked before me.

God Appears

Let us acknowledge the LORD; let us press on to
acknowledge him. As surely as the sun rises, he will
appear; he will come to us like the winter rains,
like the spring rains that water the earth.

HOSEA 6:3

~

I am not aware of much these days. I pray to be
perceptive of how You move through me and around
me. I need these signs of Your activity in my life. Much
escapes my attention. I am slow to catch what people
are saying to me. It is only by Your grace that I get
through the days.

While in this time of hibernation, I pray to be awak-
ened to Your touch. May I notice it in the rising sun
and the life-giving rains. These are not only symbols
of hope, but are also evidence of Your active presence.
This is a truth I so desperately need to hold on to.

Know When to Stand Firm

Therefore, my dear brothers, stand firm. Let nothing move you. Always give yourselves fully to the work of the Lord, because you know that your labor in the Lord is not in vain.

1 CORINTHIANS 15:58

~

I am making slow but sure progress toward my goals. I sense Your leading and have received wise counsel from people of faith. I am giving myself over to the work You have placed in front of me, and I am thankful for it. I realize that there are times You ask me to not move. You require me to be still and stand firm.

Having an unmoving faith means I must lean against the rock of Your salvation. I cling to its strength and know the form of its power so well. My ideas change and my opinions vary, but I do not move from my life's foundation.

Healing

The Process

Blessed are those who mourn, for they will be comforted.

MATTHEW 5:4

~

I am used to taking aspirin when my head aches. I drink fizzy beverages when my stomach hurts. But when my heart aches and my life is broken, I must face the spiritual process for healing. I must release myself to mourning. Lord, I can only do this because You are my Foundation.

I give myself over to Your comfort. Giving way to the flood of sorrow is not easy for me, Lord. I like to stay in control. You know all that needs healing in my life. Reach down and inspire my healing to begin.

Looking Ahead

*I know that my Redeemer lives, and that in the
end he will stand upon the earth.*

JOB 19:25

~

When I want explanations for my circumstances or
easy fixes for my ailing life, I know that I am requesting
unnecessary things. You do not call me to "get" everything about my troubles. You do call me to trust You.
It is not with reprimands or rules that You require this
of me. It is through Your love.

I cannot be certain how this time will play out. I
do not know the answers that will come my way, or if
only more questions will fill my mind. The vision of
healing I hope for might not come to pass. You might
offer something completely different for my life.

What I do know is that, at the very end, I will experience healing as I run to You—my Redeemer.

I Will

*Heal me, O L*ORD*, and I will be healed; save me*
and I will be saved, for you are the one I praise.

JEREMIAH 17:14

⟜

I will ask to be healed, and I will be healed. I will
ask to be saved, and I will be saved. You are the One I
come to in my distress or frustration, because You are
with me in my times of fulfillment and contentment.
So I know You are with me now. Praising what You
are doing in my life feels awkward at times, because
it seems so far from a hopeful situation. Yet, I praise
You honestly and with belief that I am precious to You.

I will muster up the courage to ask, Lord. And I will
hear Your response of acceptance, love, and comfort.

Because It Is Done

He said to me: "It is done. I am the Alpha and the
Omega, the Beginning and the End. To him who
is thirsty I will give to drink without cost from the
spring of the water of life."

REVELATION 21:6

~

You started and finished all that needs to be done,
for now and for all time. There is nothing I need to
accomplish that will change or secure that. That is not
my job nor the purpose You have given to me. I am to
be in covenant with You, seeking Your presence and
following in Your way so that I honor, accept, and give
glory to the Alpha and the Omega.

Because You have done all that is required, You
offer refreshment with the water of life. There is no
need to explain my thirst, because You know all that I
experience. And as I drink to fill my need, I know there
is no cost because You already paid it.

Excuses

Forgive

Bear with each other and forgive whatever griev-
ances you may have against one another. Forgive
as the Lord forgave you.

COLOSSIANS 3:13

～

Lately, I have been blaming other people for my misery. People not even involved in my struggles are suddenly in my way or the cause of trouble. I feel frustrated by those who go about life without problems right now. I realize I cannot see what they struggle with, but in my desire to find reasons for my hurt, I want to blame other people.

Lord, where there are real grievances, please help me forgive the person and to see beyond the situation. May I never use another person as a reason to not follow Your lead.

Putting the Past to Rest

Brothers, I do not consider myself yet to have taken hold of it. But one thing I do: Forgetting what is behind and straining toward what is ahead, I press on toward the goal to win the prize for which God has called me heavenward in Christ Jesus.

PHILIPPIANS 3:13-14

~

I flip through my history as though I am looking at a photo album of past mistakes. I take the images out, one by one, and I scrutinize everything about the moment. *What was I thinking? How could I? How was I to know? I was so stupid. I should never have.* It is an endless cycle of guilt, such a waste of energy.

I pray to forget what is behind me so that I can press on toward the goal. You have a purpose for my life. When I spend my time reflecting on the past, I am avoiding the future. Do not let me waste another day focused on regrets.

Send Me

Then I heard the voice of the Lord saying, "Whom shall I send? And who will go for us?" And I said, "Here am I. Send me!"

ISAIAH 6:8

~

No more hiding—I have tried that in the past, and my problems still find me. When will I learn that it is better to stand up at the beginning and ask You to send me out into my future, Your will, and my life? I want to have the courage to say, "Send me" to You, Lord. When You are seeking hearts that long to abide by Your Word and to trust Your guidance, I want to be counted faithful.

I could hide forever. I could make up reasons why I do not want to move forward and trust Your will, but no more. Send me, Lord. Here I am.

Love

Because You Are Good

Answer me, O LORD, out of the goodness of your love; in your great mercy turn to me.

PSALM 69:16

～

Because You are good.
Because You are the Source of mercy that all the
    world longs for.
Because You are my Lord, Redeemer, and Creator.
Because You see my pain and know my deepest
    fear.
Because Your peace is a balm for my troubled soul.
Because You have been with me before I was born.
Because Your eyes see through my efforts to save
    myself.
Because You brought light to my darkest hour.
Because You are love,
    You answer my plea for mercy.

Beyond a Doubt

Know therefore that the Lord your God is God; he is the faithful God, keeping his covenant of love to a thousand generations of those who love him and keep his commands.

DEUTERONOMY 7:9

～

There have been times recently that I have questioned who You are in my life, Lord. I wonder how I can feel this way when I am a person of faith. I have even said You were unfair or unjust or unfaithful. But I know that I am like an adulterous woman who blames another for her indiscretion. I have turned from You when I needed You most.

Only now can I remove the blinders of my self-thinking and see that You are faithful, and have been all along. I notice signs of Your love and care all about me. For generations You have been a God of love to Your people. May my life become one of these stories of covenant and faith.

Bring On the Compassion

May your unfailing love be my comfort, according to your promise to your servant. Let your compassion come to me that I may live, for your law is my delight.

PSALM 119:76-77

Today I need it more than yesterday. I feel my hopefulness slipping away. A few missteps and moments of doubt now lead me to Your feet, requesting an extra dose of compassion. I know I asked just last week, but I am on a roll…or a downward spiral. I cling to the hope of Your unfailing love. Let this be my comfort when my circumstances feel cold and without reprieve.

So I ask once more, because You extend grace that is not of temporal human standards, but of eternity. Bring on the compassion, Lord.

Remember Me

Remember, O LORD, your great mercy and love, for they are from of old. Remember not the sins of my youth and my rebellious ways; according to your love remember me, for you are good, O LORD.

PSALM 25:6-7

~⁀

Remember me with kindness, Lord. See me through the lens of forgiveness that blurs my past sins and my times of rebellion with the wash of Your grace. My wrongdoings are transformed by my Creator's eye for renewal. Remember me as I was that day I first met You…unsure of myself but certain of You and Your love. Forgive me when I can only recall my transgressions and not the times of renewal, Lord.

I have walked in Your ways. I have loved other people with Your compassion. By Your grace, I am not defined by the mistakes that litter my past. I am a new creation. Help me and remember me with kindness.

Peace

Deaf Ears

*The LORD has heard my cry for mercy; the LORD
accepts my prayer.*

PSALM 6:9

~

They are all about me—deaf ears. My friends, my
family, the strangers I try to connect with from my place
of brokenness—nobody hears my cries. And yet each
plea, each request for kindness or effort seems so very
loud in my own head, my own heart. After each effort,
I found myself more hurt. Can I really be this invisible?

As I desperately searched for someone to see me
fully, care deeply, my own spirit reminded me to return
to You. My words might be messy, my request in need
of refinement, but Your ears are always open to my
needs. I cry for the first time out of a sense of peace. I
do not need to keep searching. Thank You, Lord. To be
heard is transforming.

The Way of Peace

Do not repay anyone evil for evil. Be careful to do what is right in the eyes of everybody. If it is possible, as far as it depends on you, live at peace with everyone.

ROMANS 12:17-18

~

With conflict in my life, there are times that I turn from a way of peace and feed the fire of tension. I offer You my harsh words and my need for personal justice, Lord. Before I extend them to another of Your children or turn judgment toward myself, give me peace.

Strengthen my steps today. Fortify my sense of love. Help me see myself as a vessel that takes in Your love and funnels it to other people. When my humanity desires to pursue unkind actions and responses, may I turn to Your Word, Your message, and be redirected to the way of peace.

Inner Storms

He got up, rebuked the wind and said to the waves,
"Quiet! Be still!" Then the wind died down and
it was completely calm. He said to his disciples,
"Why are you so afraid? Do you still have no
faith?"

MARK 4:39-40

~⌒⌒

God, I am afraid of the inner storm that brews deep within my soul, too close to the shore of my daily life. The rough waters could destroy all that I care about. Just like Your disciples, I watch You calm the seas, and yet I still do not fully believe that Your power can hold me up or subside the torrents in my spirit.

I reveal my rage to You, Lord. I see You rebuke my wild emotions. And as peace replaces the jagged edge of leftover pain, I believe that You, Lord, will hold me up.

They Are Yours

Blessed are the peacemakers, for they will be called sons of God.

MATTHEW 5:9

~⌒~

Thank You, Lord, for those You call Your sons and daughters who are peacemakers in this world of angst, fear, and self-protection. I hope to be such a person. I see how this time of personal struggle is shaping me to be a peacemaker. My heart and eyes have been opened to how much I and all people need Your peace in this earthly journey. Your peace is the foundation from which we can reach for the heavens. It is the source that lets us love when we feel empty, uncertain, or wronged.

I believe my hurts have allowed me a deeper sensitivity to the needs of other people. Please direct me to use this gift.

Meaning

Anchored in Purpose

*We must pay more careful attention, therefore, to
what we have heard, so that we do not drift away.*

HEBREWS 2:1

Give me a perceptive mind, wide eyes, and patience
to take in the lessons You have for me during this time.
I get lost in my thoughts and worries, but I feel the pull
of Your will bringing me out of this despair. You have
a reason for my life.

I do not want to be drifting away from Your words
of guidance and direction. I pray to be anchored in Your
truth and purpose so that I might discover the meaning
of each day, trial, and victory that is part of my journey.

Your Hold on My Life

*Not that I have already obtained all this, or have
already been made perfect, but I press on to take
hold of that for which Christ Jesus took hold of me.*

PHILIPPIANS 3:12

~

Your hands shaped the fabric of my soul and body.
Before I took my first steps, You saw my last ones. And
You know the condition of every step in between. As I
move forward, may my steps become stronger, bolder,
and more willing to deviate from my own way in order
to follow Your perfect will.

When I found You, Lord, Your love took hold of
me. It was the day my life was given meaning. I hold
on to that same sense of hope and significance today.

The Meaning of It All

For everything that was written in the past was written to teach us, so that through endurance and the encouragement of the Scriptures we might have hope.

ROMANS 15:4

～

Thank goodness I was not asked ahead of time if I would accept the burdens that are in my life right now. God, I know what I would have said. But even though I did not have advance knowledge of what to expect, I do have Your knowledge to carry me through each day. Your words, communicated through obedient servants over time, now serve to build me up and restore my strength.

My chance to say no would have eliminated my opportunity to say yes—yes to learning to trust You, yes to enduring the dark to reach the light, and yes to receiving the hope that gives all my days meaning.

Sentimental Value

*Jesus answered, "If you want to be perfect, go, sell
your possessions and give to the poor, and you will
have treasure in heaven. Then come, follow me."
When the young man heard this, he went away
sad, because he had great wealth.*

MATTHEW 19:21-22

~

When I read that it is difficult for a rich man to
get to heaven, I always breathe a little easier. I am not
wealthy, so this appears to be a complication far removed from me. Yet, how many items, people, and
situations do I grip because they hold great sentimental
value to me. I cannot imagine my life without these
things. They are my riches that I place between me
and heaven.

Then You say to give them over, to be willing to
sacrifice that which has great meaning and come follow
You. Lord, help me to let go of these things. I pray I
will not face a time of sorrow by only wanting to follow
after possessions or preferences. I want to follow You.

Reaching

Reaching for Dreams

May he give you the desire of your heart and make all your plans succeed. We will shout for joy when you are victorious and will lift up our banners in the name of our God.

PSALM 20:4-5

⁓

Lord, do not let me stop reaching for the dreams I have been given. While my health, thoughts, and energy seem to be spent on survival right now, I have faith in the dreams of old. You planted them deep in my being so that through the storm of distraction, these dreams are protected.

The success I envision does not involve wealth or power. My plan for success requires only that I uncover my preserved dreams and give You the glory when they are restored and realized.

Hear My Prayer

You are forgiving and good, O Lord, abounding in love to all who call to you. Hear my prayer, O LORD; listen to my cry for mercy. In the day of my trouble I will call to you, for you will answer me.

PSALM 86:5-7

I have never been one to ask for help. You know my stubbornness, Lord. You have witnessed my tight lips when I should have been asking another person for assistance, or prayer, or comfort. Do not let me fall under this spirit of isolation and independence, Lord. If others have let me down, and that is why I go it alone, release me from this restriction.

Your love anoints the one who calls out for Your mercy. My day of trouble is upon me, and I part my lips to pray out loud to You. Hear my prayer, Lord.

Touching the Garment

When she heard about Jesus, she came up behind him in the crowd and touched his cloak, because she thought, "If I just touch his clothes, I will be healed." Immediately her bleeding stopped and she felt in her body that she was freed from her suffering.... Then the woman, knowing what had happened to her, came and fell at his feet and, trembling with fear, told him the whole truth. He said to her, "Daughter, your faith has healed you. Go in peace and be freed from your suffering."

MARK 5:27-29, 33-34

～

I have learned to fear the consequences of believing, of asking for what I need, of reaching out to touch the power of love. I learn this fear from my relationships with fallible people, not from my communion with You. Teach me to release those past hurts so that I can touch, without fear, the hem of Your garment and believe in a faith that heals.

You call me "Child" because You are Abba, Father. You see my steps of faith and do not judge them, but call them worthy of healing because You love me.

Grasping for a Miracle

Moses answered, "What if they do not believe me or
listen to me and say, 'The LORD did not appear to you'?"
Then the LORD said to him, "What is that in your hand?"
"A staff," he replied. The LORD said, "Throw it on the
ground." Moses threw it on the ground and it became a
snake, and he ran from it. Then the Lord LORD to him,
"Reach out your hand and take it by the tail." So Moses
reached out and took hold of the snake and it turned
back into a staff in his hand. "This," said the LORD, "is
so that they may believe that the LORD, the God of their
fathers—the God of Abraham, the God of Isaac and the
God of Jacob—has appeared to you."

EXODUS 4:1-5

~

Moses was so afraid that nobody would believe his
authority had come from You, Lord. I am like that too.
I do not speak up about the good things You will do
in my life because I fear other people will doubt me.
Maybe I question Your power as well. I want to believe
with all my heart, Lord.

May I reach out and take the difficult situation by the
tail so You can transform my trial into a symbol of hope
and authority. Let my miracle say to everyone that You are
in control of my life. And may they believe because of it.

Giving and Receiving

What Do You Say?

*By faith Abel offered God a better sacrifice than
Cain did. By faith he was commended as a righteous man, when God spoke well of his offerings.*

HEBREWS 11:4

~

God, I give to You my burdens today. I have some
messes in my life. My collection of emotions is covered with dirt, and many pieces are chipped, imperfect.
These days, it seems this is all I have to offer anyone.
But I know that as I hand You each of these troubles,
stains, and seemingly worthless portions of a soul, You
make them splendid and shiny.

What will You say when I turn over what is in my
heart today, when I offer You all that is my life, even
though it is not much of anything—at least not yet? I
pray You speak well of these bits of my life, Lord. Speak
them into a miracle of transformation.

It Ain't Much

He also saw a poor widow put in two very small copper coins. "I tell you the truth," he said, "this poor widow has put in more than all the others. All these people gave their gifts out of their wealth; but she out of her poverty put in all she had to live on."

LUKE 21:2-4

~

I keep going back to the story of the poor widow. I feel I am her: poor in spirit, poor in energy, poor in hope right now. Yet I fumble in my pockets and look in my change jar and find a few last pennies to give to You. I walk past people who seem to have their act together and who pull out nice, crisp bills or a checkbook. I keep walking because You are there in front of me.

I can hear You saying not to look at what pours from the pockets and hearts of these men, because what I have to give is enough. It ain't much. It barely makes a noise as I release it to the pile. But somehow I know it adds up to greatness here on the altar of eternity.

By Any Standards

You see, at just the right time, when we were still powerless, Christ died for the ungodly. Very rarely will anyone die for a righteous man, though for a good man someone might possibly dare to die. But God demonstrates his own love for us in this: While we were still sinners, Christ died for us.

ROMANS 5:6-8

~

To die for someone is beyond sacrifice. I can think of people in my life that I would give my life for, but what if You threw me in a situation where I had to stand in the place of a killer, a rapist, a person who hurt one of those people I would give my life for? By any standards, that would be absurd, unexpected, completely not the normal thing to do. I could decline and say, "Who would do such a thing?"

You would.

And while this entire thought is hypothetical on my end, it is not hypothetical to You. I am that one who is capable of hurting the people You cared enough to die for. Yet, You died for me. By any standards, Lord, You are my Savior.

Give Me All That You Have

For you know the grace of our Lord Jesus Christ,
that though he was rich, yet for your sakes he
became poor, so that you through his poverty
might become rich.

2 CORINTHIANS 8:9

~

I face a time of sacrifice and loss. I seem to be forced or called to give up those things I took for granted: security, happiness, stability, and certainty, to name a few. I never considered myself rich, but I had things I could count on, things I could control. Now I must face a poverty that leads me back to my knees, begging for all that You are and have.

Lord, You gave up great wealth and power and instead, took a vow of poverty and covenant with those in Your charge. From this poverty, You offer me new riches: security, peace, certainty, and a sure faith in You.

Wholeness

Made by God

Through him all things were made; without him nothing was made has been made. In him was life, and that life was the light of men. The light shines in the darkness, but the darkness has not understood it.

JOHN 1:3-5

⌒

You make whole creations. You made my heart, my life, and my faith. Within the circle of Your love and care, these pieces of me are whole, Lord. I feel pangs, like parts of my faith are being removed or threatened. I hold my side, as if the light is going to pour out of me and never return. Some days I lie down on my couch and hug a pillow to keep my heart from moving and breaking.

In my fragile state of being, I know You gather up this creation that You made and bathe me in light and life. Slowly I will quit checking for holes and leaks in my spirit. Slowly I will believe You made a whole and perfect vessel.

The Whole Story

I will turn their mourning into gladness; I will give them comfort and joy instead of sorrow.

JEREMIAH 31:13

~

If I could look forward in time, I would see this burden being lifted. I would understand that this pang of hurt would be reshaped into joy and wisdom. I would witness Your hand lifting me up above my circumstances. Why do I get so focused on this chapter of my life that I refuse to consider the whole story?

I know that, when I lean on my faith, I give myself a chance to believe in what comes next. I want to believe that mourning turns to gladness if I just keep living this life and reading Your Word for my life. The joy of this thought, even right now, is that I want to keep pushing forward. I cannot wait to read about my brokenness turning to wholeness in this story You are telling through me.

Usher Me In

But you, dear friends, build yourselves up in your most holy faith and pray in the Holy Spirit. Keep yourselves in God's love as you wait for the mercy of our Lord Jesus Christ to bring you to eternal life.

JUDE 20-21

~

Teach me to pray in the Holy Spirit, Lord. I have started to pray in my own way, from my own starving state of being. Somewhere I started to turn back to my need for power over my own life and it has lessened my prayers. They are mere shadows of the passionate praises and cries I shouted toward heaven at the beginning of this journey.

My numbness lets me distance myself from the leading of the Spirit. Do not let me deny this power in my life, Lord. My prayers are worthless until I allow myself to stay in Your love and wait, with belief, for Your mercy. Usher me into Your presence, Lord. I pray to be made whole.

Renewal of Spirit

*Create in me a pure heart, O God, and renew a
steadfast spirit within me.*

PSALM 51:10

~⁀

Today's culture has completely lost sight of Your art
of renewal. We upgrade, replace, toss out, give away,
or tear apart and dispose of many things in our lives.
Few people take the time to restore things in the way
that You tend to our hearts.

Yet, Lord, You can take this very weary child and
see a life worthy of attention. You do not say my
spirit is not worth keeping. You do not try to pawn
my troubles off on someone else. You do not consider
removing pieces and turning me into some unrecogniz-
able "other" thing. You see the value and purpose of
my spirit. And as You cover me in grace, You restore
my spirit to such a state of shine and luster that I can
see my faith reflected in its surface.

Belief

Never Failing

You know with all your heart and soul that not one of all the good promises the Lord your God gave you has failed. Every promise has been fulfilled; not one has failed.

JOSHUA 23:14

I can read off a list of mistakes, broken promises, and unfulfilled expectations, but this list only reflects my own side of our relationship, Lord. I see Your faithfulness in every turn of my life. I struggle to remember that during my darker days or times like now, when I feel I am juggling too many responsibilities and everyone else is letting me down.

So when I am ready to complain that there is nowhere to turn, that there is nothing to believe in anymore, remind me, Lord, that You are a God who keeps His Word...to me, to my life, to this faith journey I am on.

One More Time

*Though the doors were locked, Jesus came and
stood among them and said, "Peace be with you!"
Then he said to Thomas, "Put your finger here; see
my hands. Reach out your hand and put it into my
side. Stop doubting and believe." Thomas said to
him, "My Lord and my God!"*

JOHN 20:26-28

~~

I have asked to do this a few times in my past, but
I am most certain that this time is the most crucial to
my faith, Lord. Please, can I look at the holes in Your
hands one more time? Can I approach You as Thomas
did, filled with doubt and questions and uncertainty?
It is not so much that I am on a quest for proof. I just
need assurance. I need You to calm me once again with
Your peace.

And I need You to call me on this behavior and say,
"Stop doubting and believe." I am ready to get back
to all that You have for me in this life, Lord. But can I
look, just one more time?

Just As I Believe

Then Jesus said to the centurion, "Go! It will be done just as you believed it would." And his servant was healed at that very hour.

MATTHEW 8:13

～

Lord, You give me belief, and then honor that belief with miracles every day. It is only when I waiver, when I start relying on myself or other people too much that Your touch begins to fade. Our relationship involves both of us, and I do not always hold up my part.

Today I need You so badly. I come to You with deep, abiding faith. I am in my last hour of strength for this journey, Lord. I have waited too long to give myself over to disbelief. You take my hand and lead me to a higher place where hope rushes about me and I am revived.

Morning 'til Night

Show me your ways, O LORD, teach me your
paths; guide me in your truth and teach me, for
you are God my Savior, and my hope is in you all
day long.

PSALM 25:4-5

I awaken to Your mercies, Lord. I know that I do
not get out of bed and go to work without the sus-
taining power of Your love. While my mind spins with
frustrations and possible worst-case scenarios for my
life, You calm my emotions and let me focus on the job
before me. You even help me see the needs of other
people in the midst of my own need.

I come home feeling I have actually accomplished
something—an amazing feeling that curbs my feelings
of going nowhere in my time of trial. Some nights I
cannot sleep, yet even then You are there to comfort me
and teach me patience. Each day, morning 'til night, is
such a gift when I give it over to You, Lord.

Joy

Because of Hope

Be joyful in hope, patient in affliction, faithful in prayer. Share with God's people who are in need. Practice hospitality.

ROMANS 12:12-13

~

Because my faith tells me that tomorrow will be different, I have hope. Because I have this hope in my heart, I have joy. My difficulties are not fading, nor are they being removed from my responsibilities right now, but I have joy.

When I feel I have nothing to give, You call me to extend Your love to other people, and in that act of obedience I find joy. How You are able to lift my spirit out of the depths of despair, Lord, is the greatest mystery and delight of my faith. Thank You, Lord.

Crossing Over

*Restore to me the joy of your salvation and grant
me a willing spirit, to sustain me.*

PSALM 51:12

~

I have been a reluctant child of Yours lately. I am
dragging my feet and my spirit right along with 'em.
God, I really want to have a willing spirit. I want to
draw from Your well of salvation and sip of Your mercy
and joy. I want to experience this renewal now. I just
need help crossing over from this place of apathy to
the place of belief.

Help me to watch for Your provision. Turn my feet
toward Your heart. I want to walk to You, crawl to
You—whatever it takes to cross over that line I have
created that separates me from Your joy.

Way to Joy

Finally, brothers, whatever is true, whatever is noble, whatever is right, whatever is pure, whatever is lovely, whatever is admirable—if anything is excellent or praiseworthy—think about such things.

PHILIPPIANS 4:8

~

I know the way to joy. I watch other people about me also go through their struggles, and they do not know that the way of joy exists, let alone how to get there. You give me what I need to persevere and receive the joy of eternity. I might want to gather troubles, trip over them, shove them aside, and bring them out again, but You tell me to let go of such things and turn my attention to whatever is true, noble, right, pure, lovely, admirable, excellent, and praiseworthy.

Just repeating that list, Lord, reminds me of the goodness in my life and all around me. Through the rubble of destruction, Lord, Your words and Your truth carve out the way to joy.

Something About Today

This day is sacred to our Lord. Do not grieve, for the joy of the LORD is your strength.

NEHEMIAH 8:10

~

I start out the day with steps that are heavy with grief. I feel the pressure of life on my shoulders and begin to cave toward the sidewalk. My countenance is drawn and expressionless. I see how other people respond to me and am taken aback by the reflection of my sadness in their eyes. Then, out of nowhere and straight from Your hand, a single perfect leaf rushes past my line of vision. I watch it float, taking its time. It does not rush to the ground with the weight of burdens.

It is as if I can see Your hand cradling this symbol of a new season. You let it glide in the sky, and then You gently guide it to safety. The wind on my back becomes Your gentle hand, and I know that today is sacred. It is a day in which my journey is guided to safety by Your strength and will. I give myself over to this with great relief.

Discovery

Are You Talking to Me?

A voice of one calling in the desert, "Prepare the way for the Lord, make straight paths for him."

LUKE 3:4

~

What a wonderful day...the day I discovered that You were talking to me. At first You sounded like a wise friend. The next day You sounded like my pastor. Just yesterday You were the voice of a stranger who shared from her experience in life. Lord, through these people, I am discovering Your voice and all its mercy.

Sometimes it takes me a while to understand the message. Your written Word guides me, and my heart understands what it is You are telling me. Only now can I heed the words of John to prepare the way for the Lord. I am learning to prepare the way for the Savior of my heart to rule my life. I am finally listening.

You Can Do That?

Now to each one the manifestation of the Spirit
is given for the common good. To one there is
given through the Spirit the message of wisdom, to
another the message of knowledge by means of the
same Spirit, to another faith by the same Spirit.

1 CORINTHIANS 12:7-9

~

I am amazed how You bring people together for a reason. At first I connect with people and feel a sense of camaraderie, often because of similarities—one thing that might bond us. Over time or varying circumstances, I begin to notice the differences, and how well we complement one another.

You are a God of so many mysteries. The way You work in and through people is mighty. Help me discover the beauty of the differences that I witness in other people. I long to see what You see in them and to understand how we are part of one another's journey.

Twist of Fate

The women said to Naomi: "Praise be to the L<small>ORD</small>, who this day has not left you without a kinsman-redeemer. May he become famous throughout Israel! He will renew your life and sustain you in your old age."

RUTH 4:14-15

~୬

I am surprised by the new direction of my life, Lord. Even though the point of change is rocky, I do see the fruit of this labor. I understand that other people will look at my life and be able to see Your touch of renewal and authority. Who else but You could direct this course of events and have it lead to anything wonderful?

I must praise You with each step because I hold fast to Your ways in honor of Your faithfulness. You have not left me without a redeemer. You have not left me standing alone at this juncture. I take the next steps without worry, but with eagerness to see even this hardship through to Your end.

Limitations

*Jesus looked at them and said, "With man this is
impossible, but with God all things are possible."*

MATTHEW 19:26

⁓

My life, when it seemed to be under my control,
was very limited. No wonder the unbreakable, insurmountable walls of difficulty were being built along my
path faster than I could create detours. I had no vision,
no wisdom, no power.

Only with You is it possible to go beyond my personal limitations. Only with Your strength can I defeat
the warriors or storm the castles that stand between me
and Your plan for my journey. My true destination was
impossible in the days of old. I am so thankful I discovered how limited my view of life was at that time.
May I see only the wonders ahead…the wonders that
can be achieved only with You as my God.

To learn more about Harvest House books and
to read sample chapters, visit our website:

www.harvesthousepublishers.com

HARVEST HOUSE PUBLISHERS
EUGENE, OREGON

To learn more about Harvest House books and
to read sample chapters, visit our website:

www.harvesthousepublishers.com

HARVEST HOUSE PUBLISHERS
EUGENE, OREGON